the Hero Field Guide

Volume 1

Illustrations by Matthew Osmon
Text by Matt Langdon

We created this book for our daughters. As they grow up they are going to need some heroes. As their dads, we can provide our example, our heroes, and our hopes. But we know they need more. They need heroes to be inspired by, to emulate, and to share. We want them to have heroes of all shapes and sizes, colors and ages, nationalities and genders.

And we want this for you and your kids too.

So here it is - the first field guide of heroes to help your children (and ours) get started creating their own collection of personal heroes.

Matt & Matt

Matthew Osmon has been creating caricatures since high school when he used to draw his teachers and chapel speakers. He lives and teaches art in Flint, Michigan. He loves waiting till the last minute to make artwork. This book is no exception.

Matt Langdon has been helping kids become heroes since 1994. He lives in Australia most of the time and Michigan some of the time. He loves discovering new heroes and eating good chocolate.

If you would like to suggest a hero for the next volume, please visit
herofieldguides.com

Dedicated to Ada and Vienna

Bayard Rustin

Bayard was raised by his grandparents in Pennsylvania. They introduced him to many people involved in the civil rights movement and he helped whenever he could. After college, he learned about pacifism and nonviolence through the words of Thoreau and Gandhi. He put it into practice by protesting separate seating on interstate buses, World War II, and segregated dining in prisons.

His first big moment came when he organized the Journey of Reconciliation to test the new laws against discrimination on interstate buses. Blacks and whites rode buses across southern America and were often beaten and arrested. This got him a lot of attention and he started working with Martin Luther King, Jr., eventually convincing him to protest nonviolently. Bayard became the obvious choice to organize the March on Washington due to his skills and successes. He accomplished all of this despite many people discriminating against him for being a gay man. He was a man of integrity and stuck with his values even when it hurt him.

"We need in every bay and community a group of angelic troublemakers."

Irena Sendler

Irena was living in Warsaw, Poland during the occupation by Germany in World War II. When the Jewish people were confined to the Ghetto, she was determined to help the children, knowing that so many people were being sent to death. As an employee of the Social Welfare Department, she was allowed to enter the Jewish Ghetto. Irena built a team of people to begin saving children by smuggling them out of the Ghetto, hidden in ambulances, carts, and even sometimes disguised as packages.

Each child was given to a foster family under a different name. She kept a list of all of the children's real names buried in her garden, knowing she would need it after the war in order to reunite the children with their families. Irena's group was responsible for saving 2,500 children. In 1943, Irena was arrested by the Gestapo and tortured. She gave up no information, despite having her legs broken, and was sentenced to death. Her team saved her life by paying bribes. Irena went into hiding - listed as being executed.

"Every child saved with my help is the justification
of my existence on this Earth, and not a title to glory."

Chad Lindsey

Chad was waiting for his train on the New York subway when he noticed a man get woozy and then fall onto the tracks. The man hit his head hard and passed out. Chad dropped his bag and jumped down to try to help. The man was bleeding heavily, so Chad tried to lift him onto the platform. The height of the platform made this difficult for him to do all alone. Then he saw the lights of the oncoming train reflected on the tracks.

He remembered the story of Wesley Autrey, who lay under a train to save someone's life, and he said to himself, "I'm not doing that!" He called out for help from the previously unmoving bystanders on the platform. Some of them grabbed the arms of the unconscious man and pulled him out. Chad jumped up on to the platform ten seconds before the train arrived! He spoke to the police and then got onto the next train. He wanted to stay anonymous.

"We need to decide as human beings whether we're going to be in a moment or take a picture of it."

Sophie Scholl

Sophie and her brother, Hans, became members of the Hitler Youth before World War II, thinking that they were supporting a man who would lead Germany to a bright future. They soon realized how very wrong they were. Sophie was the youngest of a small group of friends who started discussing what could be done about the actions of their government. Speaking out against the Nazi Party was dangerous, so they created a leaflet to spread around their school campus. They named themselves The White Rose.

The first leaflet was a success - its bold message was a shock to everyone who read it. The group created five more leaflets and started a graffiti campaign with messages like, "Down with Hitler!" When the sixth leaflet was printed, Sophie and Hans brought a suitcase full of them to their university, spreading them out in the hallways while students were in class. Sophie decided to throw the last dozens of leaflets off the top of the staircase, letting them float down to the floor. Unfortunately someone saw her and most of the White Rose group was arrested. She was sentenced to death, along with her friends. All through the trial and up to her execution, she stayed calm and never backed down from her cause.

"Somebody, after all, had to make a start. What we wrote and said is also believed by many others. They just don't dare express themselves as we did."

David Shepherd & Travis Price

David and Travis were twelfth graders at a Canadian high school. At the end of the first day of school they heard about a ninth grade boy who had been crying. This boy had spent his first day of high school being teased by a group of twelfth graders for wearing a pink polo shirt. They had called him gay and threatened to beat him up.

David and Travis decided they would not stand for that sort of behaviour in their school. They planned to unleash a sea of pink the following day. Using the internet and their phones they urged everyone to wear something pink to school. The two boys purchased dozens of pink shirts, handing them out at the front door the next day. Out of a school of 1,000 students, 800 came in pink! When Travis and David saw the boy who had been bullied, the smile on his face rewarded them more than they could have imagined. Pink Shirt Day is now celebrated around the world every year.

"We're not heroes,
we're just two kids who stood up for a cause."

Chiune Sugihara

Chiune worked for the Japanese government in Lithuania. His job was to grant visas to people wanting to travel to Japan. It was not usually a very busy job. That changed in 1940 when Nazi Germany took over Lithuania during World War II. News of the Nazis' treatment of Jews had spread, so many Jewish people were desperate to escape Europe. Hundreds of people started arriving at Chiune's door, looking for a way out. He saw their need and their fear, so he contacted his superiors, asking for advice. They told him, three times, not to give out visas to these people. After speaking with his family, he decided to risk his job, his freedom, and his life, by writing as many visas as he could.

Chiune wrote the visas by hand, spending every waking hour on them. He was now writing the same number of visas in a single day that he used to write in a month. Finally, his consulate was closed due to the escalating war. He stayed awake with his wife all through their last night, still writing visa approvals. He continued frantically writing visas in the taxi to the train station, and was throwing visas into the crowd through the train's window as it pulled out.

"Please forgive me. I cannot write anymore.
I wish you the best."

Ethan King

Ethan visited Mozambique with his dad when he was ten years old. He took his soccer ball because he knew kids in Africa loved soccer, and he hoped to find some friends to play with. He got more than he bargained for when dozens of kids showed up to see a real soccer ball. They'd grown up playing with balls made of plastic bags wrapped with twine. At the end of Ethan's visit he gave his ball to the kids in the village. They were overjoyed.

On his trip home Ethan couldn't stop thinking about the looks in the eyes of those kids. By the time he got back to Michigan, he had a plan. He launched a nonprofit called Charity Ball, which is dedicated to providing new, quality soccer balls to kids living in poverty. His first call for a donation ended with a "no", but he persevered. Charity Ball now provides thousands of balls every year to children all over the world.

"You don't have to be famous and you don't have to be a specific age to help someone."

Aung San Suu Kyi

Both of Aung San Suu Kyi's parents were politicians, and she spent much of her youth and early adulthood living and learning in different countries. At age 43, now a wife and mother of two sons, she returned to Burma to lead the fight for democracy. At the time, the military ran the country, having taken control by force. The military leaders offered Aung San Suu Kyi freedom if she would agree to leave Burma forever. She chose to sacrifice her freedom to remain true to her cause and her country. She lived under house arrest for fifteen of the next twenty-one years as a result.

She was rarely allowed visitors, not even from her husband and sons living overseas. The military regularly encouraged her to leave the country, but she knew that she would never be allowed back in. Even when her husband died in England, she chose to stay in Burma rather than attend his funeral because her cause was everything to her. During her entire imprisonment she followed and promoted the nonviolent philosophy she'd learned from Mahatma Gandhi. In 2010, she was finally released.

"You should never let your fears prevent you from doing what you know is right."

Vincent Lingiari

Vincent was a Gurindji man in northern Australia who worked at the Wave Hill cattle station. Aboriginal workers were badly paid and sometimes not paid at all. Frustrated by the inhumane conditions, Vincent led two hundred of his people away from Wave Hill in a 'walk-off,' demanding better pay, better rations, and protection of the Aboriginal women. They sat in peaceful protest at Wattie Creek.

The fight for better working conditions transformed into a campaign to have their tribal lands returned. Eight years of protest later, Prime Minister Gough Whitlam poured red earth into Vincent's hand to show that the government was giving back 3,300 square kilometres to the Gurindji people. Finally, his people were able to work their own land.

"We want to live on our land, our way."

Malala Yousafzai

Malala loved school when she was a young girl. Her father encouraged her, despite the ruling Taliban's ban on education for girls. When she was eleven years old she started writing an anonymous blog for the BBC in England, where she described her life under the Taliban. The next year an American documentary team filmed her daily life, after which she became famous in and out of Pakistan for promoting the education of girls. Her fame over this controversial topic attracted death threats from the Taliban. One morning the threats became a reality, as a man boarded her school bus and shot her in the face.

She survived.

After spending two and a half months recovering in an English hospital, Malala chose not to hate. She didn't blame the man who shot her. She didn't hate the Taliban. She just continued fighting for what she believed in - education for every child in the world.

" I speak not for myself,
but so those without a voice can be heard."

Andree de Jongh

"I knew what needed to be done.
There was no hesitation.
We would not stop
What we had to do
although we knew the cost."

As a child, Andrée's hero was Edith Cavell, an English nurse who helped rescue British troops during World War I. As an adult volunteering for the Red Cross during Word War II, Andrée had the chance to mimic her hero. Many British soldiers found themselves trapped behind enemy lines in Belgium. Andrée created a network of safe houses and secret paths to transport soldiers to Spain, where they could be sent to England. Over 800 Allied troops escaped using the Comet Line (named for its speed). Andrée personally led 118 of them.

No one thought she could do it. Not the people in Spain, not the people in Belgium, and certainly not the soldiers. She was too young, too small, too pretty. "Our lives depend on a schoolgirl," said one Australian soldier. When she was finally caught by the Nazis she was interrogated twenty times before she finally confessed to being the leader of the Comet Line. Her captors laughed at her because they wouldn't believe such a little woman could do so much. She was sent to prison and survived the war. Instead of living as a hero in Belgium, she went to Africa to help in leper colonies.

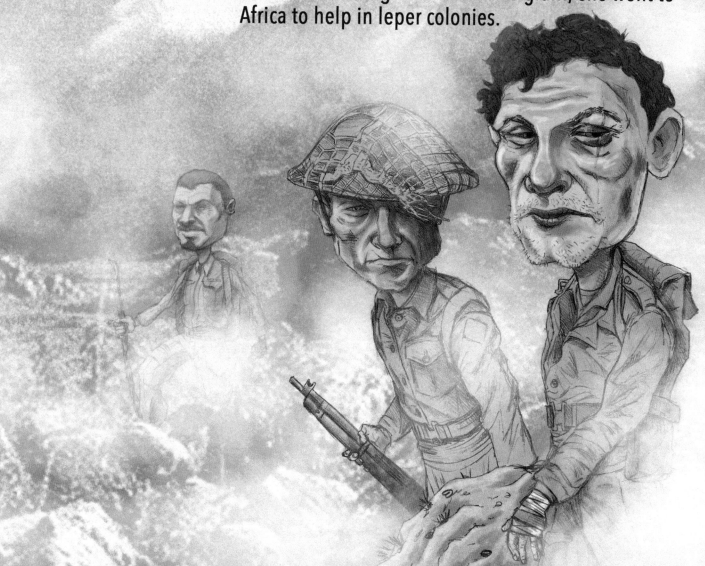

Carlos Arredando

In 2004, on his birthday, Carlos learned that his son had died while on duty in Iraq. While battling his own grief, he chose to campaign for peace rather than sit in anger. The empathy he developed in talking to so many people in pain was soon put to good use.

In 2013, Carlos was attending the Boston marathon when a bomb went off near the finish line. While many people watched in shock or fled, Carlos ran to the blast site to help move debris and help the injured. He saw a young man with his shirt on fire and immediately beat out the flames.
Noticing that the man's legs had been destroyed by the bomb, Carlos lifted him onto a wheelchair and tourniqueted one leg. He and a woman wheeled the victim to an ambulance, saving his life.

"I was in a state of shock briefly,
and then I realized I needed to help."

Irene Morgan

Feeling sick and tired on a bus ride to a doctor's visit, Irene refused to give up her seat to a white couple. She was already in the black half of the segregated bus. The driver drove straight to a police station, where an officer boarded the bus and gave Irene a warrant for her arrest. Irene tore up the warrant and kicked the deputy sheriff, saying she was within her rights.

She was arrested and pleaded guilty to resisting arrest, paying a $100 fine and apologizing for her violent behavior. But she refused to pay the $10 fine for sitting in the wrong seat. She appealed, and her case caught the attention of Thurgood Marshall, who took the case to the Supreme Court. They won. Her actions inspired others to stand up to injustice, including those on the Journey of Reconciliation led by Bayard Rustin. Eleven years later, Rosa Parks famously refused to give up her seat on a bus.

"I can't see how anybody in the same circumstance could do otherwise."

Iqbal Masih

Iqbal was sold by his family to a carpet maker when he was four years old. Millions of families were forced into this kind of arrangement in Pakistan due their extreme poverty. He was kept, with many other children, in cramped conditions and forced to weave carpets all day. He was even chained to his loom at times.

One day, Iqbal snuck away from the carpet factory with some other children and ended up at a freedom celebration. He heard from numerous speakers that slavery was illegal. At that moment, he decided he would never return to his owners. He joined up with the Bonded Labour Liberation Front and began speaking at similar events, despite being threatened by carpet company owners. His example was enough to inspire thousands of other children to leave their owners. He spoke so well, that he was asked to give a talk in the United States and his message spread around the world. At age twelve, he was assassinated by men hired by the leaders of the carpet industry.

"I would like to do what Abraham Lincoln did... I would like to do it in Pakistan."

Dolores Huerta

Dolores was raised by her mother in a farming town in California. Her mother's hotel gave her the opportunity to meet people of many backgrounds as she was growing up. She also spent a lot of time as a Girl Scout, learning many skills. After graduating as a teacher, Dolores was concerned by the poor conditions many of her students lived in. Instead of teaching them, she decided to help their parents.

With Cesar Chavez, Dolores created the National Farm Workers Association. She taught farmers to organize themselves into groups so they could demand improvements from politicians and business owners. In all of the protests, Dolores encouraged nonviolence, even after she was badly beaten by police in San Francisco. Her work also inspired women around the country, so she started focusing on women's rights. Dolores has improved the lives of millions of workers and women by speaking up for them.

"Every moment is an organizing opportunity, every person a potential activist, every minute a chance to change the world."

Desmond Tutu

Desmond was trained as a teacher, but has spent most of his life as an Anglican bishop in South Africa. He organized peaceful protests against the harsh apartheid laws that saw blacks being treated as second class citizens. He risked prison and violence throughout this time in South Africa. He also traveled the world, encouraging other countries to stop trading with South Africa as a way of pressuring them to change the laws. In 1994, apartheid finally ended after decades of effort.

Since then, Desmond has fought against inequality all over the world. He has worked to eradicate HIV and other diseases in Africa as well as supporting gay rights, church reform, women's rights, and much more. He also founded the Elders, a group of world leaders who try to create solutions to problems around the world. Despite the seriousness of his work and the risk involved, Desmond is famous for his broad smile and sense of humor.

"If you are neutral in situations of injustice, you have chosen the side of the oppressor."

herofieldguides.com